Hello!!

This is just a quick message to say THANKS! for purchasing me and having me in your busy life!

There are different pages in here for you to colour in and doodle on, designed in ways you may not have seen before.

I really hope I can make you relieve some tension and stress in your life and I hope that this journey will be one to be remembered and to see this as a good hobby to keep going on with, both with fun and lots of creativity!!

Enjoy! Bye for now...

Find and colour in the names of the animals

Hippopotamus   Gorilla   Crocodile
Ostrich   Zebra   Koala
Tiger   Lion   Camel
Rabbit   Elephant   Cat
Kangaroo   Panda   Chimpanzee
Snake   Giraffe   Lemur
Antelope   Dog

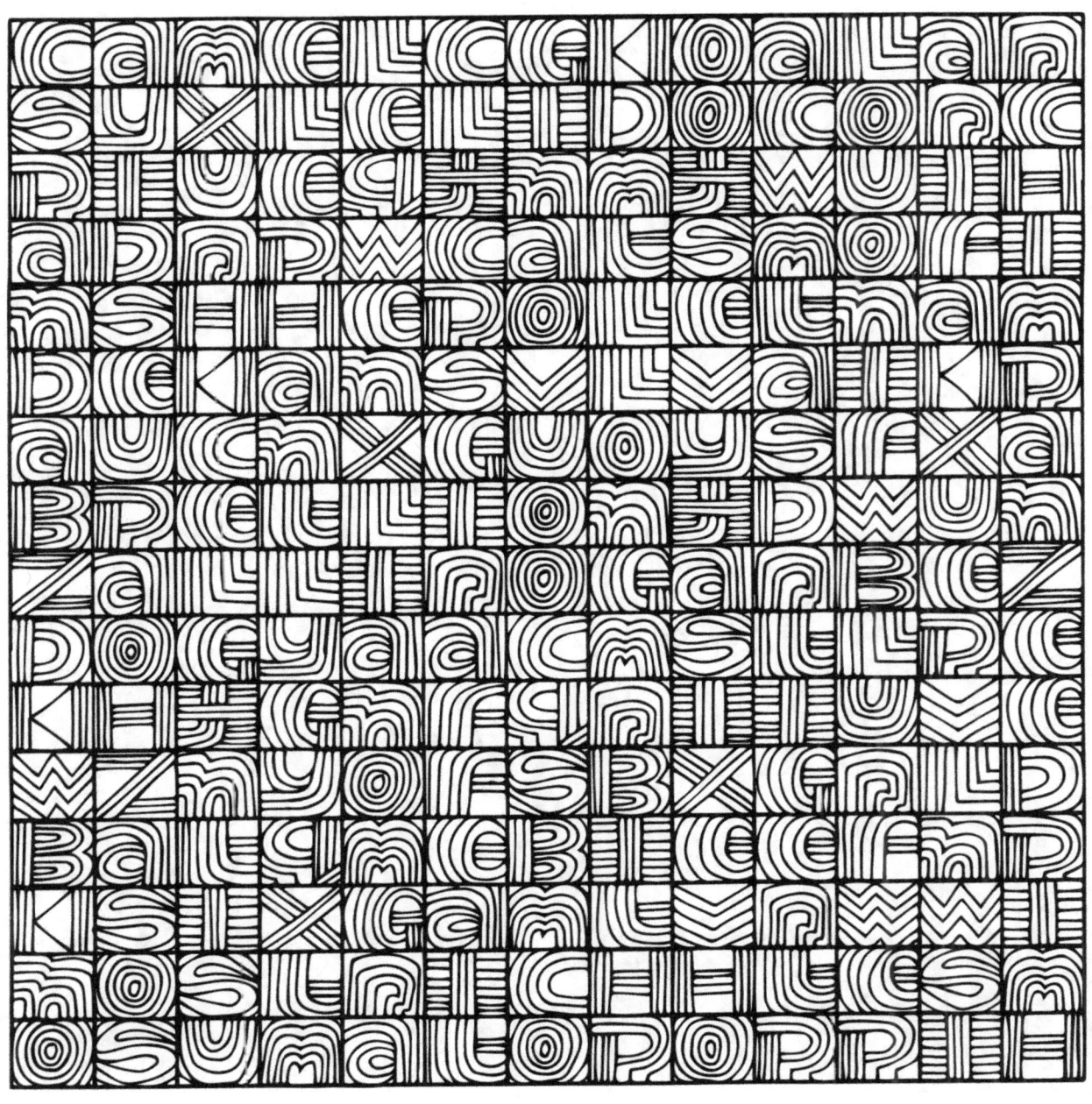

Oh Hello again! As you can see this is a blank page, well, apart from this text you are reading of course! Show this page what you can do by drawing or colouring anything you like on here, start anywhere on the page and just work your way through!

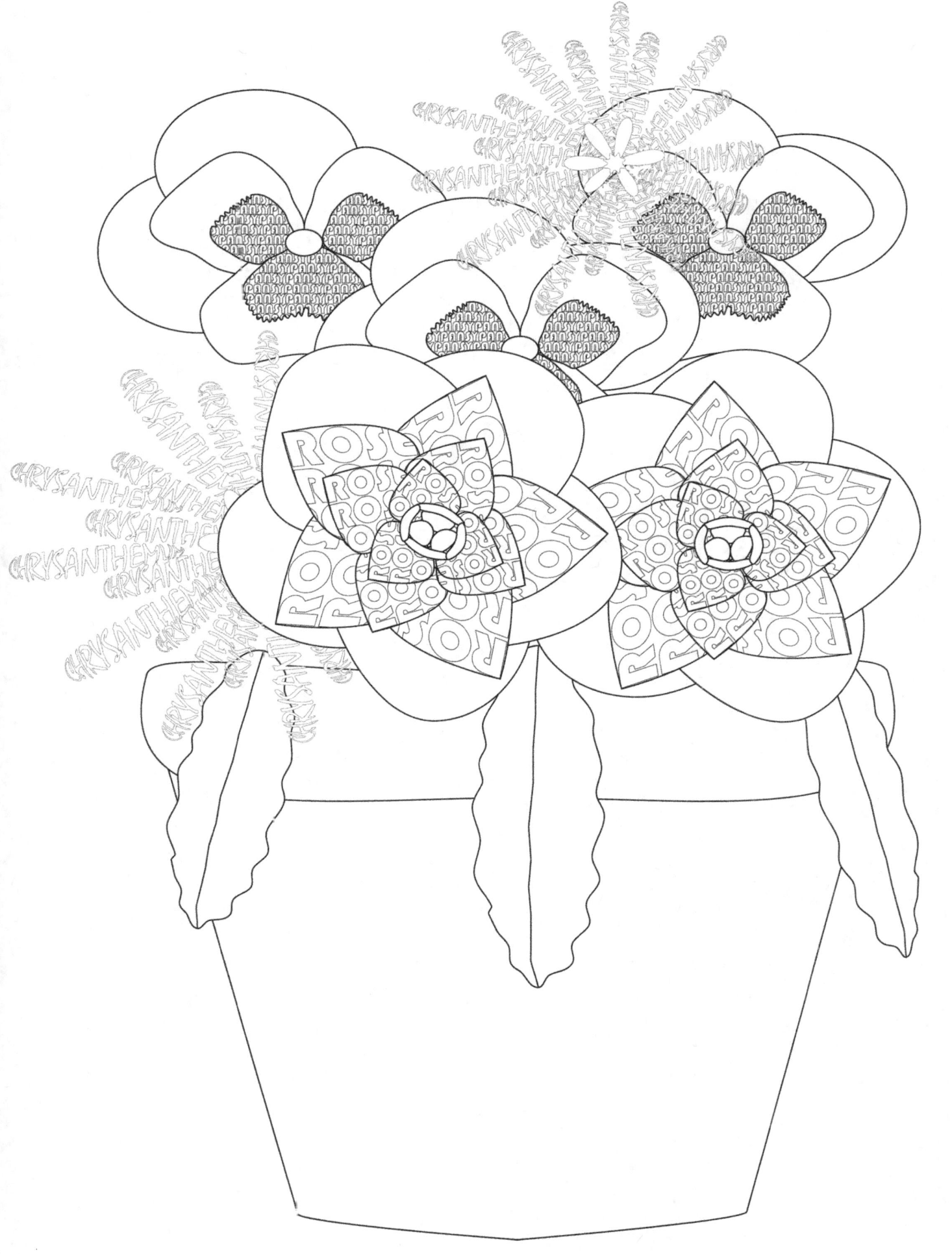

Don't forget that I am here for you, to be creative with, if you feel like taking your mind off from the rest of the day! Be strong and be bold, you will get through it. Feed your hands with your drawing urge and fill this page with your designs, paintings, sketches, anything you like that will take your mind away from the stresses of life...

Find and colour in the names of the cars

Chrysler   Lexus   Bentley   Saab

Mercedes   Jaguar   Honda   Nissan

Renault   Chevrolet   Toyota   Alfa Romeo

Citroen   Fiat   Vauxhall   Volkswagen

Peugeot   Audi   Mitsubishi

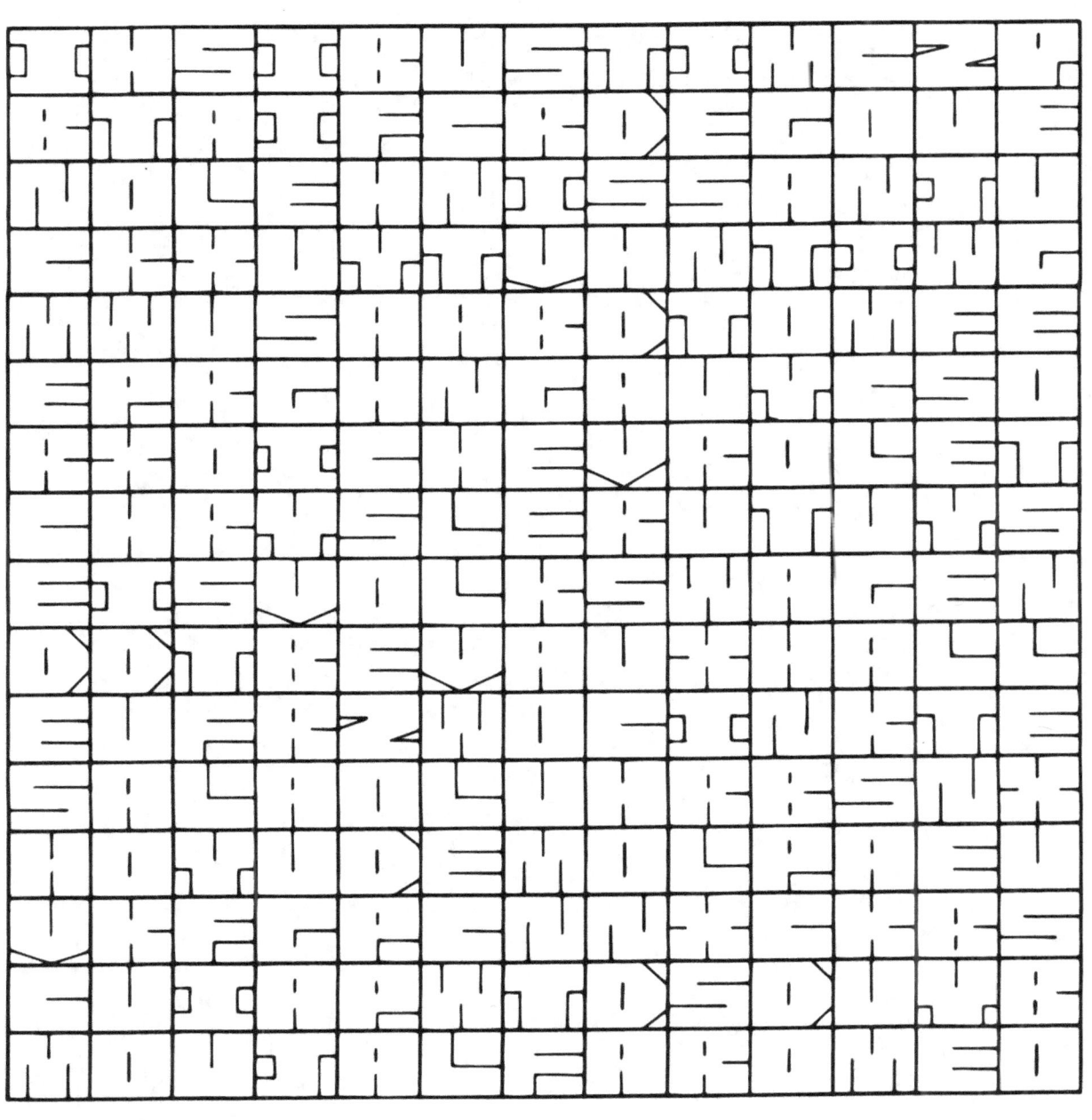

Always keep your head up high, think of the positive things you have in your life as these will overcome the negatives. Take a deep breath, release all that tension and channel it all on these pages in any way you like, be it colouring, writing, just plain doodling, anything you like!

Thank you for purchasing this book and I hope you thoroughly enjoyed it!

Please check out my website for my other works and information on future publications - https://elainemcnay.wordpress.com

www.ingramcontent.com/pod-product-compliance
Lightning Source LLC
Chambersburg PA
CBHW081546280526
45788CB00010B/3373